You Na Brussels Sprouts You!

Recipes for the Devotee

Keith Pepperell

DEDICATION

To my spawn Jack, Lydia, and Alex all of whom are fond of a sprout or two

ACKNOWLEDGMENTS

Sprout Lovers Everywhere
Sprout Scholars Everywhere
Lady Estima Davenport
Muriel Dinwiddy
World Sprout Association
Hirohito Fong

Rüdiger Wölk, Münster

Velvet
Woollard End Brussels Sprout Growers
Association
Professor E. W. Quimbush-Merkin
Jennifer McLagan
Jane Grigson
Mark R. Vogel

1. BRUSSELS SPROUT BIOLOGY

The Poor Widow Brussels-Sprout

The naughty Brussels sprout also known
as brussels sprout is the common name
for a cultivar group, Brassica oleracea

Gemmifera Group, of the wild cabbage (B. oleracea) of the mustard family Brassicaceae (or Cruciferae). This plant is a hardy cool season biennial, and its sexy axillary buds develop along the stem into small, cabbage-like heads. The term *Brussels sprouts* is used for these edible, leafy, green buds, which have become naughty little foods of desire.

The rascals are native to mostly coastal southern and western Europe. Their ancient ancestors were commonly claimed to have been cultivated in Ancient Rome and vegetable expert Pfyffer suggests possibly as early as the 1200s, in

Belgium.

The earliest written description of Brussels sprouts was claimed by noted sprout scholar Folsom to have been in 1587. It is plausibly argued Brussels sprouts were popularly cultivated as a vegetable crop in the 1500s in Belgium and their popularity later expanded into other temporate countries.

Brussels, according to Mills (2001) are likely a mutant of the plucky savoy cabbage B. oleracea capitata, L. sabuda subgroup.

Further, noted food writer Jennifer

McLagan presents a scholarly account of Brussels sprout history when she reports English food writer Jane Grigson, points out they are first mentioned in the city of Brussels's market regulations in 1213. This would suggest they were being grown in the Low Countries at that time. However, not until two centuries later do they appear again, this time on the menus of Burgundian wedding feasts held at the court of Lille. At that time the powerful dukes of Burgundy controlled northern France and most of the Low Countries. After this appearance on the royal table, Brussels sprouts vanish again; it seems they were never a popular vegetable, or perhaps they remained a very local specialty.

In the late eighteenth century they resurface, this time in gardening books rather than cookbooks. "Brussels sprouts are winter greens growing much like boorcole" is how they're described in Charles Marshall's *Plain and Easy Introduction to Gardening* (1796). This shows that it was the leafy green tops of the plant that were popular, not the small buds attached to the thick stem. Thomas Jefferson is often credited with bringing Brussels sprouts to America. While he did plant them in his garden at Monticello in 1812, it is debatable whether this was their first appearance in the New World. They may well have arrived earlier with the French settlers to Louisiana, some of whom came from northern France.

However, it was their popularity as a garden plant that returned them to our tables, at least in England. By the mid-nineteenth century Elizabeth Acton, in her *Modern Cookery for Private Families* (1845), was explaining how to cook them Belgian style, boiled and smothered in butter. As a young woman, Elizabeth had spent time in France, where she had no doubt eaten them. A few years later in 1849, French chef Alexis Soyer included a recipe in his book *Modern Housewife.*"

Brussels sprout biologists like Mills in scholarly descriptions inform "Brassica olearacea var. gemmifera is a cool season biennial, with axillary buds produced in the leaf axils during the first year of growth and a seed head produced in the second year of growth.

The stems are light grayish green in color, with the axillary buds produced beneath the leaves in the nodes of the elongated stem.

The roots are shallow, with eighty percent of the roots growing in the upper eight to twelve inches of soil. The simple, alternate leaves are round to heart-shaped with long petioles; they are light green to deep grayish-green in color."

And further "The flowers are perfect (with male and female parts) and borne in terminal racemes. Flowering is stimulated by temperatures below 45 degrees Fahrenheit for one or two months."

The flowers are pollinated by naughty insects.

There are numerous cultivar varieties in the United States that include "Catskill" (or "Long Island Improved," a dwarf variety with medium sprout size), "Jade Cross" (compact variety with medium size sprouts), "Early Morn Dwarf Improved" (dwarf variety), "Breda" (taller, earlier cultivar type), and "Red Vein" (later maturing, more hardy cultivar).

Noted sprout scholar Mark R. Vogel finds the etiology of Brussels sprout at best tricky. He writes, "It never ceases to amaze me how many foods and classic recipes have histories embroiled in mystery, controversy and general contrariety. Most of the time when researching a particular comestible, I find myself lost in a universe of permutations. Consider the etiology of something as seemingly simple as the Brussels sprout. After reviewing five textbooks, an encyclopedia, and a well known food history website*, I was able to determine that Brussels sprouts originated in Europe in either the 5th, 13th, 15th, 16th, 17th or 18th century. Well that narrows it down.

 What is known is that cabbage, the ancestor of Brussels sprouts, is indigenous to the Mediterranean and has been cultivated for at least 2,500 years. Cherished by the ancient Greeks and Romans, it was propagated by the latter throughout Europe. Whatever the temporal period, Brussels sprouts were cultivated in Belgium and hence were eponymously named after its capital city. The French introduced them to Louisiana in 1800. Today most American Brussels sprouts hail from California and end up in

frozen products. Interestingly, despite their

Belgian roots, the Netherlands are the key

producer in Europe."

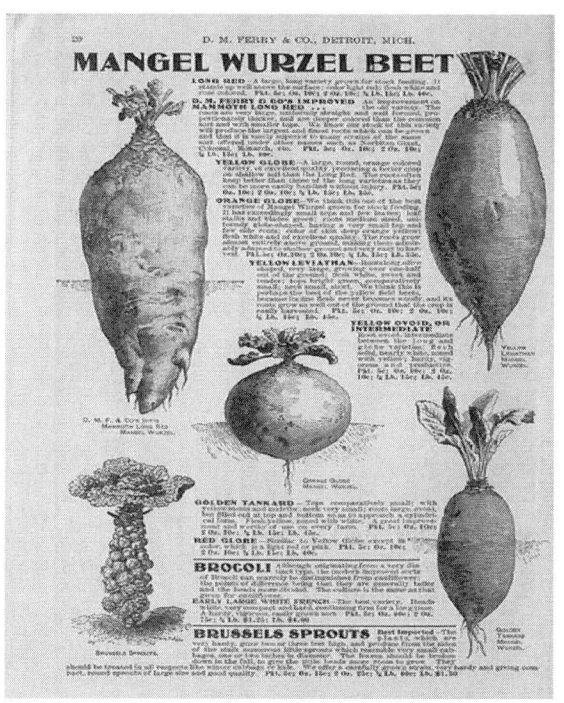

Poor Little Brussels Sprouts (l) Menaced by
a Gang of Punk Mangel Wurzel Beet

Gardening expert Bonnie L. Grant tells us

poor little Brussels sprouts are prone to specific pests and diseases. Generally, they are prone to those pests suffered by other types of cabbage plants including aphids, maggots, earwigs, cutworms, leaf miners, nematodes, republicans, attorneys, realtors, snails and slugs

She suggests protection methods including, "Protect young plants from cutworms but putting a collar around the plants. You can prevent flying insect damage with a net or row cover over the crop. Practice crop rotation to avoid some of the common insect larvae that live in soil and feed on foliage and roots. Use organic pesticides to combat severe infestations and "pick and crush" larger pests. The best defense from Brussels sprout pests is healthy plants. Make sure they get adequate water and plant in well-drained soil in full sun. Plants with good vigor can more easily withstand minor infestations from Brussels sprout pests."

Ms. Grant also advises, "Bacterial and fungal diseases are the primary Brussels sprouts problems. Some of these just discolor or mar foliage but others can cause defoliation. This becomes a problem in large amounts because it affects the plant's ability to photosynthesize.

Bacterial diseases spread quickly and thrive in moist areas. Minimize overhead watering and remove affected plants. Similarly, fungal issues thrive in damp conditions.

Some fungus survives in debris over the winter. It is a good idea to remove all old plant material, which may harbor spores.

Molds, like white mold and downy or powdery mildew, can be prevented by drip irrigation and good plant spacing.

Most diseases affecting Brussels sprouts are easy to prevent with good cultivation and care practices."

Gang of Cunning Aphids Up To No Good
In terms of cultivation, the tall variety of

Brussels sprouts stands between two and

four feet tall and the short variety grows

to a maximum of two feet.

The rascal Brussels sprouts grow best,

according to canny horticulturalists, in

temperatures between 45 and 75°F with

optimum yields with highest yields grown

at 60 to 65°F. Commercially, Brussels

sprout plants grow from seeds in and are

transplanted to large growing fields and

can be harvested at 90-180 days. As I was

stated ante, edible sprouts grow like buds

on the side of the stalks. Sprouts may be

picked by hand most often 5 to 15 sprouts

at a time, by cutting the entire stalk

(attractive and presently quite popular in

localstores stores). Mechanical harvesters are also used and may be more commonly employedas non-citizen labor is methodically deported under this administration. A single stalk will produce 2 1/2 to 3 although somewhat less in commercial harvesting. European consumers including the author prefer smaller sprout sand Americans larger ones.

European production has historically been considerably greater than in the United States with the Netherlands, (where it is suggested the industry first flourished) Germany, and England as the largest producing nations.

Cultivation of Brussels sprouts in the United States has grown since its inception in the very early nineteenth century in Louisiana via the French. Commercial production began in the United States in about 1925 in the Louisiana Delta later moving t o mid-coastal California, New York and Washington .

Presently sprout scholars report that about 80 to 85 percent of U.S. production is for the awful frozen food market, wherein the sprouts taste so bad that only non-knowlegable Americans would ever think of eating them.

Chou de Bruxelles demi-nain de la Halle.
Réd. au dixième; pomme à demi-grandeur.

2. BRUSSELS SPROUTS AND NUTRITION

Brussels sprouts are low in calories and high in nutrients and further, Brussels sprouts are high in protein for a naughty green vegetable, and a single serving, for meets vitamin C and K daily needs.

As stated ante, Brussels sprouts are a part of the cruciferous family including broccoli, cauliflower, kale cabbage, and collard greens all of which supply many nutrients for a small calorie content. The health benefits of Brussels sprouts are very well documented and are among the twenty most nutritious foods in in terms of their vitamin, mineral, and phytonutrient content in relation to caloric content.

One cup of raw Brussels sprouts (about 88 grams) provides only 38 calories, 0 grams of fat, 8 grams of carbohydrate (including 3 grams of sugar and 2 grams of fiber) and 3 grams of protein.

Consuming one cup of Brussels sprouts will provide 195 percent of vitamin K, 125 percent of vitamin C, and 10 percent or more of the daily vitamin A, vitamin B-6, folate, potassium, and manganese needs.

Accordingly, there are many health benefits associated with Brussels sprouts consumption particularly in reducing obesity, heart disease, and diabetes. It is also well-established that Brussels sprout eating contributes towards increased energy, healthier skin, and weight loss.

Further, the sulforaphane content that give cruciferous vegetables their bitterness at the same time gives them their cancer-fighting power. Sulforaphane also inhibits the production of the harmful enzyme histone deacetylase. Brussels sprouts also contain "a high amount of chlorophyll, which can block the carcinogenic effects of heterocyclic amines generated when grilling meats at a high temperature." Adequate vitamin K consumption improves bone health by acting as a modifier of bone matrix proteins, improving calcium absorption, and reducing urinary excretion of calcium. Brussels sprouts are high in vitamin K content.

Brussels sprouts also contain an extremely useful antioxidant that has been shown to lower glucose levels, increase insulin sensitivity, and prevent stress-induced changes in patients with diabetes.

Brussels sprouts are high in vitamin C which assists in eye health and eyes including protection against UV light damage.

Brussels sprouts also contain the antioxidant zeaxanthin — that filters out harmful blue light rays.

The natural vitamin c content in Brussels sprouts also can help to fight skin damage caused by the sun and pollution, reduce wrinkles, and improve overall skin texture.

Vitamin C also plays a vital role in the skin supporter collagen production.

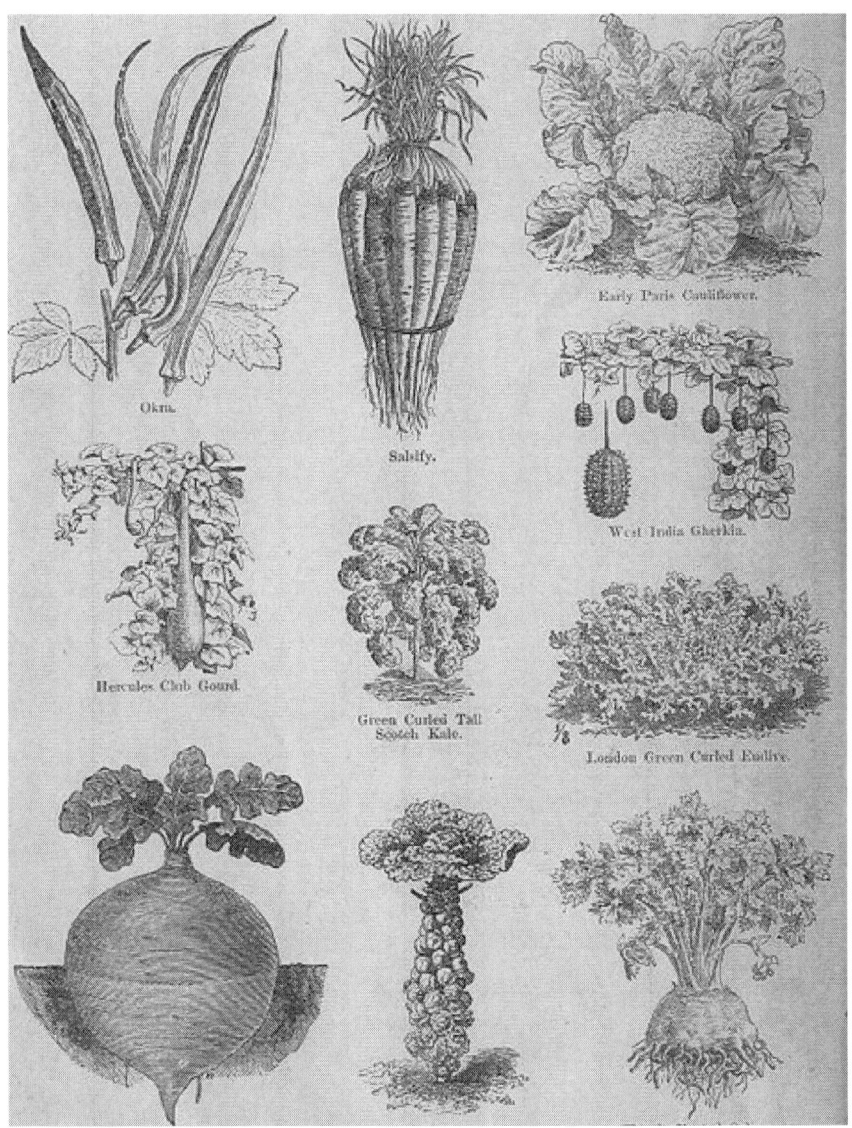

Brussels sprout Stalk Very Cleverly
Impersonating a Nuclear Explosion
(Bottom Center)

Nutrition Facts

Brussels Sprouts(one cup)

Calories 38	From Fat 6%
From Carbohydrates 74%	From Proteins 20%

Frozen Brussels Sprouts available in the Market(4 ounces)

Calories 46	From Fat 8%
From Proteins 24%	From Carbohydrates 68%

Cooked Brussels Sprouts(4 ounces)

Calories 46	From Fat 8%
From Proteins 24%	From Carbohydrates 68%

Creamed Brussels Sprouts(One cup)

Calories 194	From Fat 50%
From Proteins 14%	From Carbohydrates 36%

Keith Pepperell

Amount Per 100 grams ▾

Calories 43

		% Daily Value*
Total fat 0.3 g		0%
Saturated fat 0.1 g		0%
Polyunsaturated fat 0.2 g		
Monounsaturated fat 0 g		
Cholesterol 0 mg		0%
Sodium 25 mg		1%
Potassium 389 mg		11%
Total Carbohydrate 9 g		3%
Dietary fiber 3.8 g		15%
Sugar 2.2 g		
Protein 3.4 g		6%
Vitamin A	15%	Vitamin C	141%
Calcium	4%	Iron	7%
Vitamin B-6	10%	Vitamin B-12	0%
Magnesium	5%		

3. BRUSSELS SPROUTS AND 'HUMOR'

Sadly, there are many truly awful Brussels sprout gags and almost all of which are not the least bit amusing. The author remembers many of them from his schoolyard days. I am sure those who first contrived the following stinkers would be delighted to remain anonymous. Here are some in all of their vileness,

"Q: What can you call a Brussels sprout that smell worse than a skunk?

A: Pepe le Sprout.

Q: Did you hear about the weightlifting

vegetable?

A: He was a muscle sprout.

Q: What vegetable eliminates the need to brush your teeth?

A: Bristle sprouts!

Q: What do you call kids who eat their vegetables?

A: Brussels sellouts.

Q: What water yields award winning Brussels sprouts?

A: Perspiration!

I call my Brussels sprouts.....cabbage patch

kids.

Q: What do you call kids born in whorehouses?

A: Brothel sprouts.

Q: What do you call vegetables found underwater?

A: Snorkel sprouts.

Q: What is the worlds least selling beer?

A: Brussels stout.

Q: What is green and goes to summer camp?

A: A Brussels' scout!

Q: What kind of socks do you need to wear when you plant Brussels sprouts?

A: Garden hose!

Q: What do you get when you cross Brussels sprouts with a popular snack?

A: Pretzel Sprouts.

Q: What vegetable can you eat for dessert?

A: Streusel sprouts.

Q: What do you get when you cross Brussels sprouts and a jackhammer?

A: Chisel sprouts.

Q: What do you call vegetables that don't get along?

A: Quarrel Sprouts.

Q: What is the difference between Brussels sprouts and snot?

A: Children will eat their snot!

Q: What do you call the screams of little kids when you tell them to eat their veggies?

A: Brussels shouts.

Q: What do you call vegetables singing in church?

A: Gospel sprouts.

Two Brussels Sprout Buddies

One day two Brussels sprouts, who were best of friends, were walking together down the street. They stepped off the curb and without warning a speeding car came around the corner and ran one of them over.

The uninjured Brussels sprout immediately called 911 and helped his injured friend as best he could. The injured Brussels sprout was rushed to ER and straight into surgery.

After a long and terrifying wait, the doctor finally appeared. He told the uninjured Brussels sprout, "I have good news, and I have bad news. The good news is that your friend is going to pull through." "The bad news is that he's going to be a vegetable for the rest of his life".

In the Doctors Office

A guy walks into the doctor's office.

A banana stuck in one of his ears, a Brussels sprout in the other ear, and a carrot stuck in one nostril.

The man says, "Doc, this is terrible. What's wrong with me?"

The doctor says, "Well, first of all, you

need to eat more sensibly."

I warned you they were awful, with perhaps the exception of the nasty snot gag.

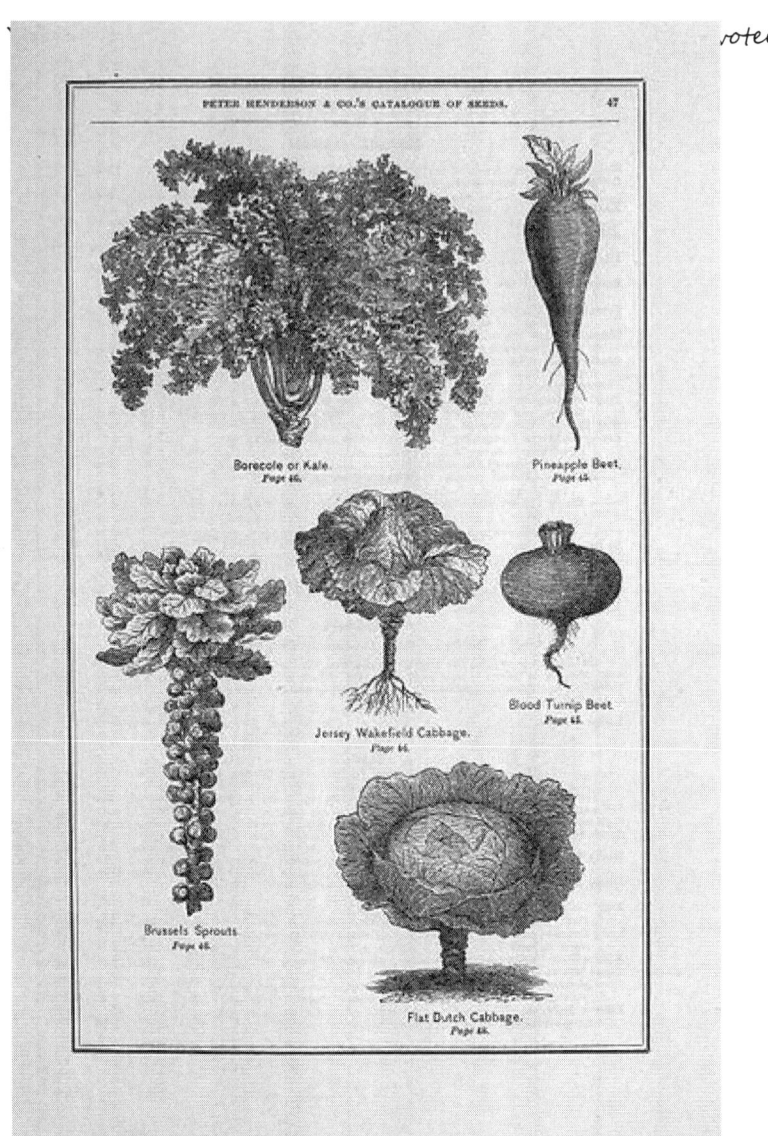

Naughty Vegetable Girly Book

4. BRUSSELS SPROUT RECIPES

Such is the present popularity of this naughty superstar vegetable ,that there are a wondrous number of most excellent recipes commonly presented. Some of the author's favorites are set out post.

There are some interesting Brussels sprout quotations that include ,

"A fruit is a vegetable with looks and money. Plus, if you let fruit rot, it turns into wine, something Brussels sprouts never do."

{P. J. O'Rourke}

"The flesh on the nape of my neck did the crawly thing that it does so well. Some

people say this is God's warning that the devil is near, but I've noticed I also experience it when someone serves me Brussels sprouts."
{Dean Koontz}

"We kids feared many things in those days – werewolves, dentists, North Koreans, Sunday School – but they all paled in comparison with Brussels sprouts."
{Dave Barry, Miami Herald }

Certainly, Brussels have not enjoyed the best of reputations, largely as a result of their being almost always 'cooked to death'.

The most excellent chef and food writer

Mark M. Vogel writes in The Reluctant Gourmet, "Brussels sprouts have an unjust reputation for mawkishness. Many people who dislike them have only been exposed to improperly stored or cooked Brussels sprouts. While I'm sure some will recoil even under the best circumstances, you owe it to yourself to revisit them under ideal conditions.

First they must be fresh. Brussels sprouts grow on stalks and sometimes supermarkets will sell them with the stalks attached. Clearly this is preferable. If sold loose or worse yet, in pre-wrapped packages, inspect them carefully. If the leaves are yellow, discolored or loose, or if the root ends are brown or appear dry, avoid them altogether. If possible, choose smaller specimens as they are tenderer than their big brothers. Once purchased, endeavor to use them promptly. Do not hold them beyond three days in the fridge or they can develop off flavors. On yet another disparate note, some sources advise storing them in a plastic bag and others do not. Just use them expediently and bypass this contention."

1. LADY ESTIMA DAVENPORT'S BRUSSELS SPROUTS WITH BACON,

DRIED FRUITS & ALMONDS

If there had ever existed a modern-day monstrous regiment of women Lady Estima Davenport would, most certainly, have been its Colonel-in-Chief with her old school chum and championship winning tennis partner Muriel Dinwiddy as her able subaltern. Indeed immediately following the first blast of a Knoxian trumpet either lady would have instantly seized it and poked it ungraciously into the blowhard's bottom.

INGREDIENTS

¼ cup best dried cherries

¼ cup currants

1 cup dry white wine (drink the rest quickly)

1 lb. nice freshly picked firm Brussels sprouts

8 slices best bacon very thinly sliced

¼ cup finely slivered almonds

A little splash of favorite balsamic vinegar

Kosher or nun-blessed salt & white pepper to taste

Best olive oil as required

METHOD

Preheat the oven to 375 degrees. F Place the cherries and currants in a saucepan and add the wine. Drink the rest of the bottle Bring to a gentle boil and remove from the heat. Let the fruit steep in the lovely hot wine for about twenty minutes or so. The fruit can sometimes be heard singing naughty barrack room ballads Carefully trim the naughty Brussels sprouts avoiding severing a limb or cutting an artery. Slice off the course, woody root ends. Then cut them in half vertically discarding any outer leaves. Remove any of the wanton remaining outer leaves that are discolored or aphid and other insect nibbled. Once cut, wash them, drain, and pat dry.

Combine all of the ingredients except the olive oil in a bowl and toss them vigorously . Then, gently and slowly add the olive oil evenly but lightly moisten everything. The lovely bacon w drippings will weave their magic web. Place everything in a baking dish and cook in the oven for about 25 minutes or so. Delightful!

2. AUNTY MURIEL'S SPICED AND ROASTED BRUSSELS SPROUTS

In 1924 Aunty Muriel Dinwiddy had clouted Winston Churchill with her handbag. Churchill was Chancellor of the

Exchequer at the time under Stanley Baldwin whom Muriel despised with a passion. She had once quite vulgarly claimed at a rally that he was "living proof that sodomy could produce children." She was promptly arrested, thrown into a black maria, and later fined ten shillings at the Bow Street Magistrates Court.

It transpired Baldwin had enraged Muriel when he had spoken of 'the impracticability of socialism.'

Estima had flown at Churchill during a rather posh dinner at the Mansion House calling him 'a boggle eyed piss artist'. This occurred soon after Britain's disastrous return to the gold standard resulting in unemployment, deflation, and the miners' strike that precipitated the General Strike of 1926. Some mashed potatoes had also been propelled in Winnie's general direction.

On another occasion, while in her cups, she had bellowed to Winnie "call yourself a boozer, I could drink you under the table with both of my hands tied behind your back." Muriel is well-known for her deadly use of kitchenalia during WW II against the evil Hun and her Brussels sprout recipes.

INGREDIENTS

1½ pounds nice fresh tight Brussels sprouts

½ cup extra-virgin or not very naughty olive oil

¼ cup Chinese rice-wine vinegar

¼ cup local honey

2 tablespoons Sriracha,

Kosher or nun-blessed salt and freshly ground white pepper

METHOD

Preheat the oven to 400°F. Trim the

woody base away from the Brussels sprouts

and throw at an annoying neighbor. Cut

the naughty sprouts in half.

In a large bowl, whisk the not very

naughty olive oil with the Chinese rice-

wine vinegar, honey and Sriracha and

combine these nicely. Add the Brussels

sprouts and toss quite vigorously until

they are all moist and fully coated.

Season well with salt and white pepper

Spread the naughty Brussels sprouts

seductively on a baking sheet, flat sides

down. Pour any remaining olive-oil

mixture onto the pan and lovingly distribute it. Sometimes the sprouts will purr gleefully.

Roast until the sprouts are nice and crispy on the outside and all a lovely golden brown and caramelized on the flat sides, about twenty five minutes or two gin and tonics should do nicely. Serve these tasty rascals immediately.

3. Dr. PINKY LECTER'S BRUSSELS SPROUTS KILLER LATKES

INGREDIENTS

1 small yellow onion carefully cut in half

1 large peeled potato

1 pound fresh, tight Brussels sprouts, trimmed and finely shredded

2 nice big brown locally sourced eggs, lightly whisked

1 egg white, lightly whisked

⅓ Cup of all-purpose flour

Kosher of Nun-Blessed salt and ground white pepper

Olive oil

Some nice Himalayan salt, for finishing

Sour cream

METHOD

Grate the yellow and remove excess moisture. Transfer into a large bowl.

Grate the potato and squeeze out the moisture and place to the bowl with the onion.

In the large bowl, toss the onion with the potato and Brussels sprouts to combine. Stir in the eggs, egg white, flour, salt and pepper, and mix until all nice and happy together

Heat about 1 inch of oil over medium heat. Scoop in several ½ cup batches of the naughty Brussels sprouts mixture into the hot oil. Flatten slightly. Cook until all nice and golden and crisp. About four minutes a side should do nicely.

Repeat until all the latkes are made. Serve immediately, garnished with a little Himalayan salt and a drizzle of the sour cream. Lovely.

4. DON LUIGI'S CHEESE OVERCOAT PARMESAN SPROUTS

INGREDIENTS

1/2 cup favorite olive oil

1 cup Panko crumbs

1/3 cup freshly grated best Parmesan cheese

1 tablespoon Cajun seasoning

1 pound Brussels sprouts carefully trimmed

1/2 cup all-purpose flour

2 large locally sourced brown eggs beaten

METHOD

Heat the vegetable oil in a skillet over medium high heat.

In a bowl, combine the Panko crumbs, Parmesan and the Cajun seasoning and reserve

Working in batches, dredge the Brussels sprouts in the all-purpose flour, dip into eggs and then dredge in Panko mixture until all nicely coated.

Drink some Chianti

Add the naughty Brussels sprouts to the skillet, 5 at a time, and cook until all lovely and evenly golden and crispy, 3 minutes should suffice.

Transfer to a paper towel-lined plate and then serve immediately.

Fabulous for friends of ours.

5. LYDIA EDGECOMBE-PEPPERELL'S BRAISED BRUSSELS SPROUTS WITH HARD APPLE CIDER

INGREDIENTS

3 strips best bacon cut into small strips crosswise

2 tablespoons best salted butter butter

1½lbs. best fresh, firm Brussels sprouts, trimmed and halved

2 large shallots, roughly chopped

1 cup hard apple cider (drink the rest swiftly or Lydia will)

1 tsp. Locally sourced fresh honey

1 tsp. kosher or nun blessed salt

Ground white pepper

METHOD

Heat a cast iron skillet over medium-high gas. Add the bacon strips and cook, stirring until all lovely and until brown and crisp. Remove the bacon and drain. Pat dry.

Pour all but 1 about a tablespoon of bacon drippings in a nice glass jar and reserve for another use. Add best salted butter to skillet. When the butter has melted, add the naughty Brussels sprouts. Cook for about 5 minutes, gently agitating the skillet to prevent burning. Dancing helps but take care.

Stir in the shallots and cook for 3 minutes. Add the cider, honey, salt and pepper, gently mix, and bring to a boil. Serve immediately while drinking several more ciders. Make sure Lydia doesn't head-butt you.

6. PROFESSOR LARRY 'KNUCKLES' EDWARDS' CHEDDAR BRUSSELS SPROUTS

INGREDIENTS

2 -3 lbs best fresh firm Brussels sprouts

2 -3 lbs best fresh firm Brussels

sprouts

1/4 cup best salted butter

1/4 cup all-purpose flour

1 cup chopped yellow or white onion

2 cups warm milk

1 1/2 cups shredded white cheddar cheese (divide into two)

1/2 teaspoon kosher or nun-blessed salt

1/2 teaspoon ground white pepper

1 teaspoon ground nutmeg

METHOD

Parboil the Brussels sprouts for 7 minutes and drain.

Place into a 2-3 quart oven proof dish.

Saute the onion in butter until clear and then add the all-purpose flour and stir.

Drink a beer

Add the warm milk, nun-blessed salt, white pepper, nutmeg, 3/4 cup cheese and stir.

Pour filling over the naughty Brussels sprouts.

Top with remaining 3/4 cup

cheese and bake at 375 for 40

minutes or so.

Sparklingly good!

7. QUIMBUSH MERKIN'S VERY NAUGHTY BALSAMIC AND CRANBERRY BRUSSELS SPROUTS

This recipe was handed down by Ophelia Merkin, a striking woman and only daughter of the late Professor Quimbush Merkin an Oxford don and Shavian scholar. She was Chairperson of The Mid-Suffolk Lady Bicyclists Association.

Professor Merkin was a noted cross-dresser and market gardener whose

Brussels sprouts were frequent prizewinners at The Woollard End Village Fete and Hog Roast.

INGREDIENTS

3 pounds fresh firm cleaned Brussels Sprouts

1/2 cup Extra virgin or slightly naughty Olive Oil

Kosher or nun-blessed salt and ground white pepper

1 cup Balsamic Vinegar

1/2 cup Sugar

1 cup Dried Cranberries

METHOD

Trim and clean the naughty Brussels sprouts, then cut them in half if Arrange on two baking sheets and toss vigorously with the best olive oil. Sprinkle with plenty of salt and ground white pepper and roast at 375 degrees for 30 minutes, or until brown.

Drink two beers.

Combine balsamic vinegar and sugar in a saucepan. Bring to a rolling boil then reduce to medium-low and reduce until very thick, about 20 minutes should do nicely.

Drizzle the balsamic reduction over the

lovely naughty roasted sprouts, then sprinkle on dried cranberries. Toss and serve immediately. Drink several beers.

8. LADY JOAN PEPPERELL'S BRUSSELS SPROUTS CAESAR SALAD

INGREDIENTS

4 cups thinly sliced firm fresh cleaned Brussels sprouts

1 Tbsp. Mayer lemon juice

2 tsp. Finely chopped chives

2 tsp. finely chopped parsley

1/4 cup freshly grated Parmigiano-Reggiano cheese

3 Tbsp. dressing

For the dressing:

1 egg

Juice of one Mayer lemon

2 oil-packed anchovies

2 garlic cloves, minced

1 Tbsp. whole grain mustard

1/4 cup extra-virgin or slightly naughty

olive oil

Kosher or nun-blessed salt and ground

white pepper

METHOD

To make the dressing, whisk everything

together in a medium bowl and set aside

Drink a nice glass of very chilled white wine

To make the salad, shave the Brussels sprouts with a mandolin, or very thinly slice with a knife, crossways. Combine all of the ingredients in a bowl and mix lightly with your hands. Garnish with more grated cheese. Drink more wine

9. 14th CENTURY MENAGIER DE PARIS DISH OF BRUSSELS SPROUTS

ORIGINAL RECEIPT: Eileen Power's translation

And when the heart of the cabbage, which is in the midst, is plucked off, you

65

pull up the stump of the cabbage and

replant it in fresh earth, and there will

come forth from it big spreading leaves;

and the cabbage takes a great deal of room

and these cabbage hearts be called Roman

cabbages and they be eaten in winter; and

when the stumps be replanted, there grow

out of them little cabbages which be

called sprouts and which be eaten with

raw herbs in vinegar; and if you have

plenty, they are good with the outer leaves

removed and then washed in warm water

and cooked whole in a little water; and

then when they are cooked add salt and

oil and serve them very thick, without

water, and put olive oil over them in

Lent.

MODERN RECIPE TRANSLATED FROM ORIGINAL :

INGREDIENTS

1 lb. fresh firm Brussels sprouts

water

4 tablespoons olive oil 2 tablespoons of

best butter

pinch salt

METHOD

Shell and wash the Brussels sprouts. Place in a pan and bring water to just the top of sprouts. Bring to a nice rolling boil, reduce heat, & simmer water until sprouts are tender. Drain well. Toss with olive oil or butter and salt. Serve and start conversation about monastic manuscript illumination.

10. JANET FROBISHER'S CARAMELIZED ONION AND BACON BRUSSELS SPROUTS

INGREDIENTS

4 slices best cured bacon

1/4 cup best salted butter

1 small yellow or white onion, quite finely chopped

1 teaspoon firmly packed brown sugar

1 $1/2$ pounds fresh, firm Brussels sprouts, trimmed and halved

DIRECTIONS

Cook bacon in a nice clean medium non-stick skillet until all lovely and crispy. Drain. Crumble; set aside. Discard bacon drippings or save for later in refrigerator.

In the same skillet, melt the butter over a medium heat; add onion and sugar. Cook for about 10 minutes, stirring occasionally, until onions are all lovely and moistly tender and caramelized.

Pace the naughty Brussels sprouts in 3-quart saucepan; add 1 inch of water. Bring to a rolling boil over medium-high heat. Cover; and reduce heat to lowish and then cook for about nine minutes until tender. Drain well.

Add the Brussels sprouts to onion in skillet; toss vigorously to coat. Cook over a medium heat until heated through. Sprinkle with the lovely bacon. Drink three beers. Delicious!

Displaying Lady Brussels Sprout with
Aroused Gentlemen Asparagus
Nearby

ABOUT THE AUTHOR

Little is known of the author's
whereabouts since he is in a witness
protection program. He is probably quite

mad too.

Printed in Great Britain
by Amazon

65206479R00050